PIANO VOCAL GUITAR

ROY ORBISON
THE BEST OF THE SOUL OF ROCK AND ROLL

T0081946

ISBN 978-1-61780-778-7

HAL•LEONARD® CORPORATION
7777 W. BLUEMOUND RD. P.O. BOX 13819 MILWAUKEE, WI 53213

Visit Hal Leonard Online at
www.halleonard.com

BLUE BAYOU

Words and Music by ROY ORBISON
and JOE MELSON

Moderately

I feel so bad, __ I've got a wor - ried mind;
Go to see __ my ba - by a - gain

I'm so lone - some all the time, since I left my
and to be with some of my friends; may - be I'd be

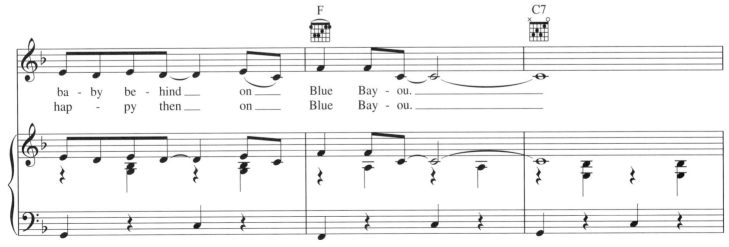

ba - by be - hind __ on Blue Bay - ou.
hap - py then __ on __ Blue Bay - ou.

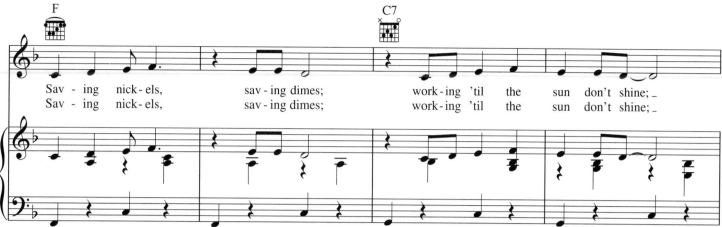

Sav - ing nick - els, sav - ing dimes; work - ing 'til the sun don't shine; __
Sav - ing nick - els, sav - ing dimes; work - ing 'til the sun don't shine; __

look - ing for - ward to hap - pi - er times __ on Blue Bay - ou. __ I'm go - ing
look - ing for - ward to hap - pi - er times __ on Blue Bay - ou. __ I'm go - ing

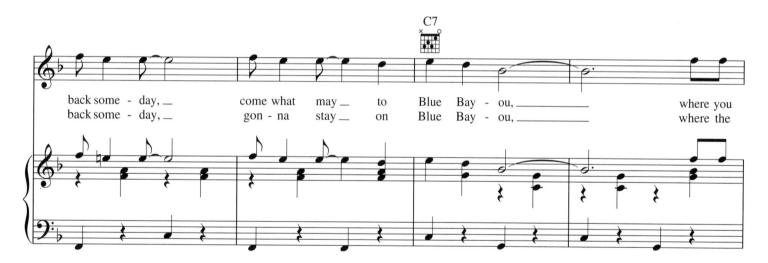

back some - day, __ come what may __ to Blue Bay - ou, _____ where you
back some - day, __ gon - na stay __ on Blue Bay - ou, _____ where the

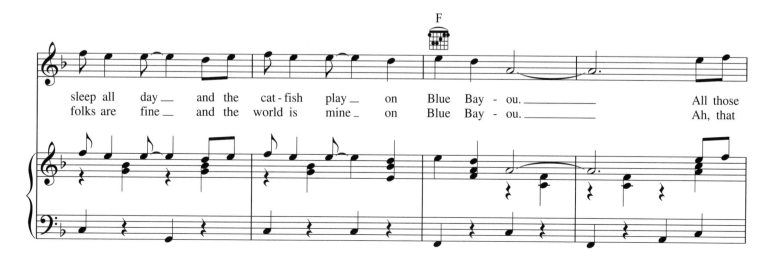

sleep all day __ and the cat - fish play __ on Blue Bay - ou. _____ All those
folks are fine __ and the world is mine __ on Blue Bay - ou. _____ Ah, that

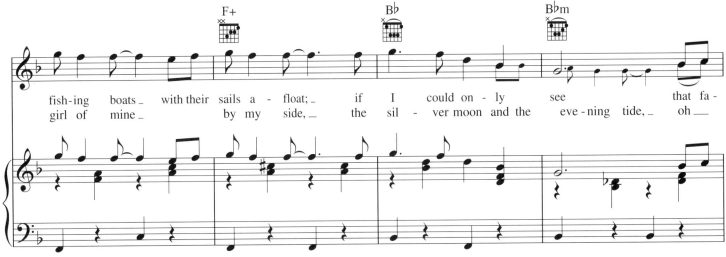

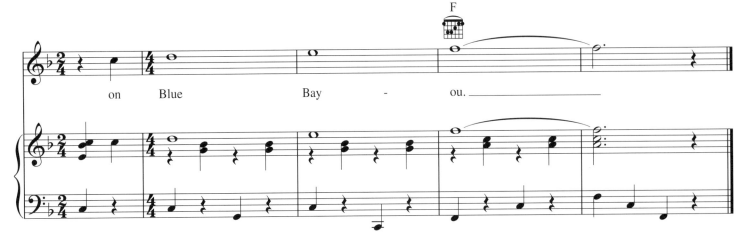

CRYING

Words and Music by ROY ORBISON
and JOE MELSON

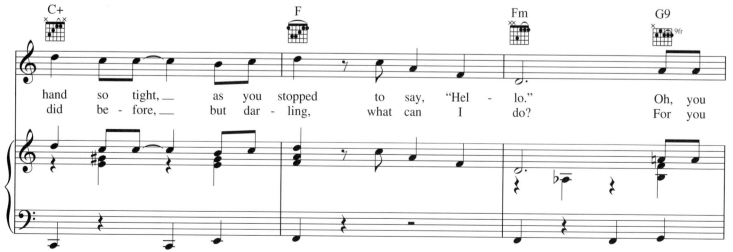

wished me well; ___ you could - n't tell _____ that I'd been
don't love me and I'll al - ways be _____

cry - ing o - ver you, cry - ing
cry - ing o - ver you, cry - ing

o - ver you. When you said, "So
o - ver you. Yes, now you're ___

long;" left me stand - ing ___ all a - lone, a - lone and
gone and from this ___ mo - ment on I'll be

(All I Can Do Is)
DREAM YOU

Words and Music by BILLY BURNETTE
and DAVID MALLOY

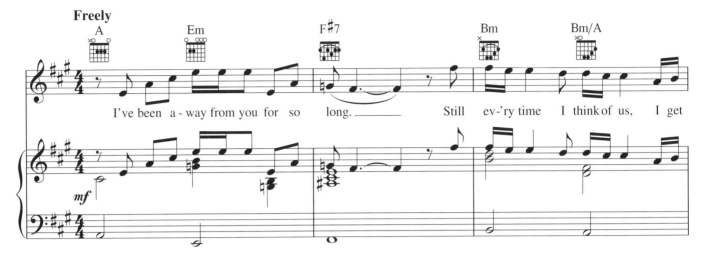

I've been a-way from you for so long. _____ Still ev-'ry time I think of us, I get

blue. _____ But all I can do _____ is dream you.

Up-tempo Rock

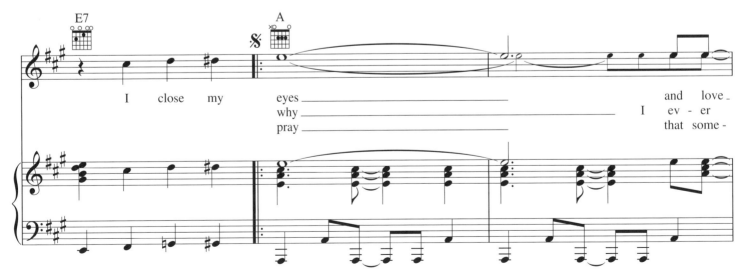

I close my eyes _____ and love _
why _____ I ev- er
pray _____ that some-

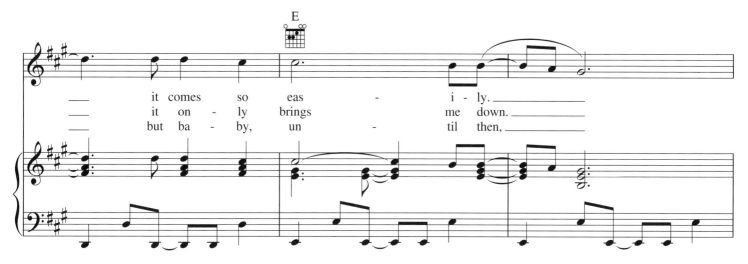

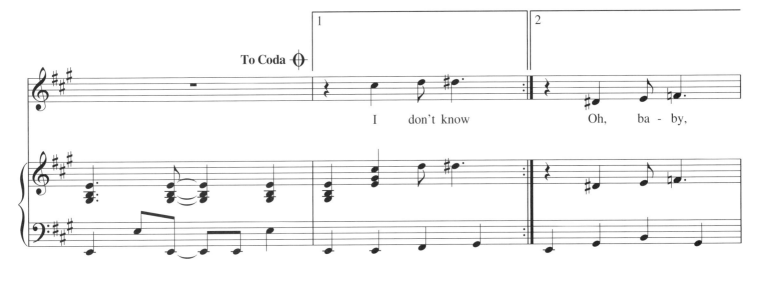

is dream ___ you. All ___ I can do ___ is dream ___ you. ___

Here I go ___

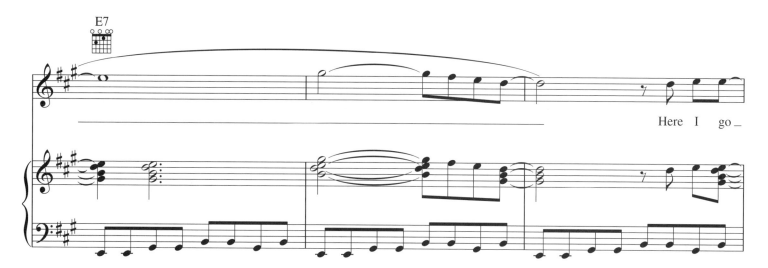

___ dream-in' you. ___

Ev-'ry day I

D.S. al Coda

CODA

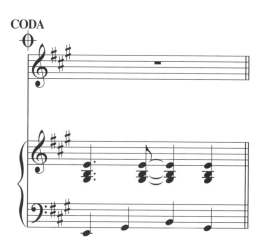

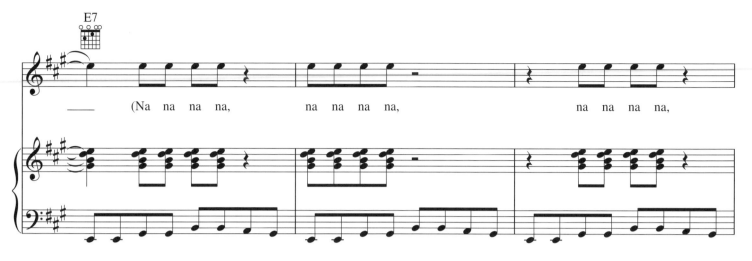

(Na na na na, na na na na, na na na na,

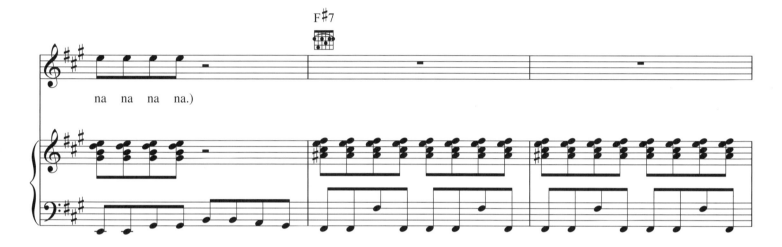

na na na na.)

(Na na na na,

na na na na, na na na na, na na na na.)

FALLING

Words and Music by
ROY ORBISON

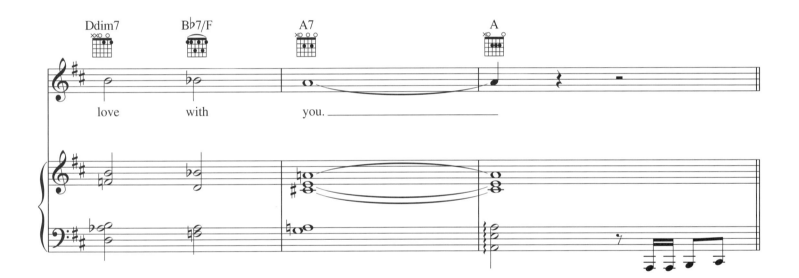

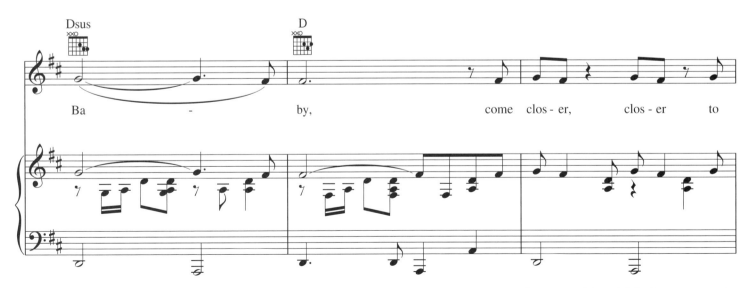

me, and lis - ten,

lis - ten so care - ful - ly: Re -

mem - ber all the nights that I told you I

love _____ you? _____ It was - n't true: I

used you, __ and you were __ just some - one new.

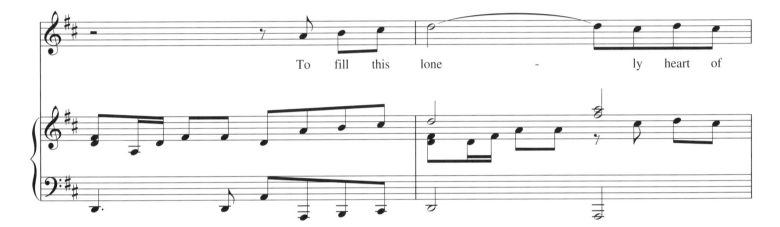

To fill this lone - ly heart of

mine, I was ly - ing all the time, pre -

tend - ing to be fall - ing in love __ with

you. _____ But it's

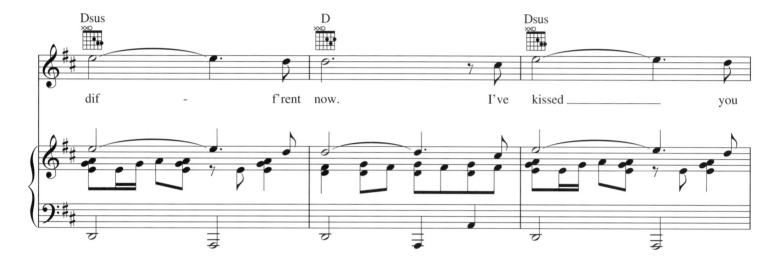

dif - f'rent now. I've kissed _____ you

now, so for - give me, for - give me some -

how. Hold _____ me

tight _____ for _____ to - night, then tell me

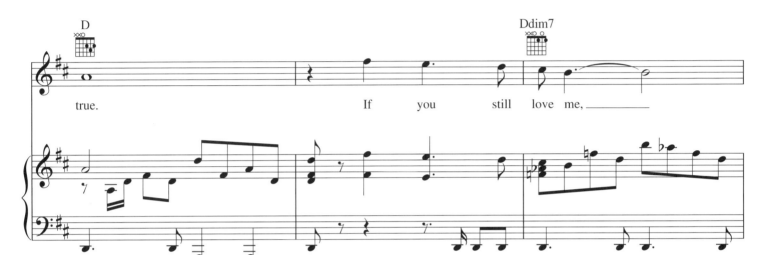

true. _____ If you still love me, _____

say that you love me. _____

Don't leave me now, _____ now that I'm fall - ing for

you. _____ I'm

fall - ing, I'm fall - ing, _____ fall - ing in

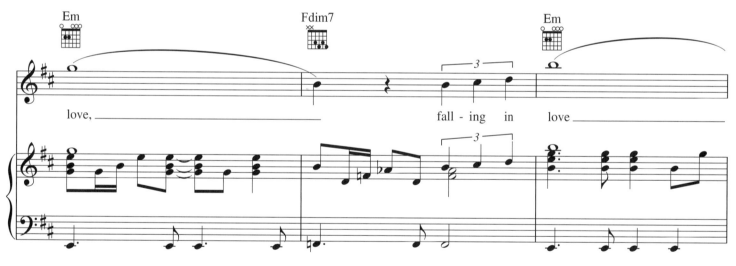

love, _____ fall - ing in love _____

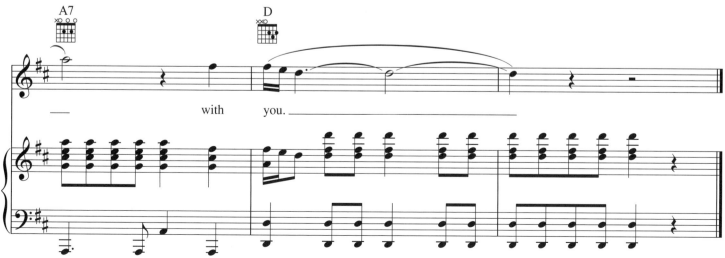

__ with you.

I DROVE ALL NIGHT

Words and Music by BILLY STEINBERG
and TOM KELLY

Moderately fast

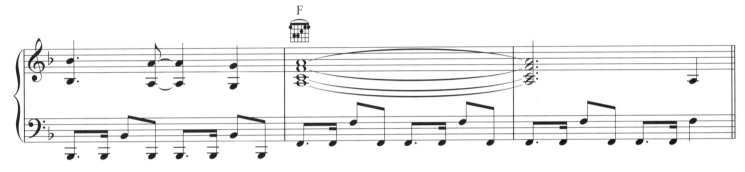

I had to es - cape. ___ The cit - y was
What in this world ___ keeps us from

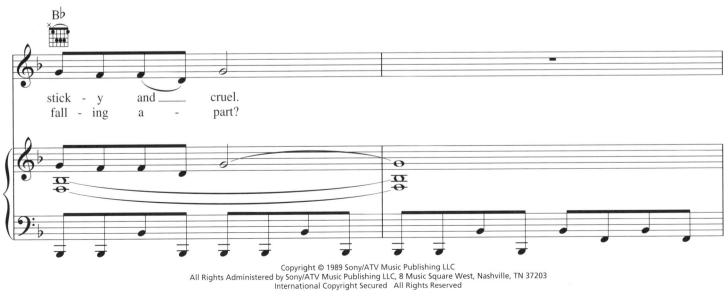

stick - y and ___ cruel.
fall - ing a - part?

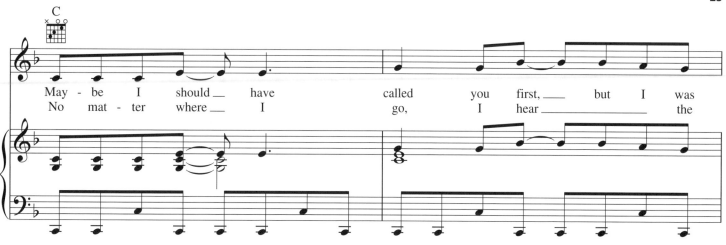

May - be I should __ have called you first, __ but I was
No mat - ter where __ I go, I hear _____ the

dy - ing to get to you. I was
beat - ing of our one heart. I

dream - ing while I drove the long, straight road __ a -
think a - bout __ you when the long night is cold __ and

head, uh - huh, yeah. Could
dark, uh - huh, yeah.

you.   Is that   all   right?

I   drove   all   night, _____   crept   in   your

room,   woke   you   from   your

sleep   to   make   love _   to   you. _____

Could

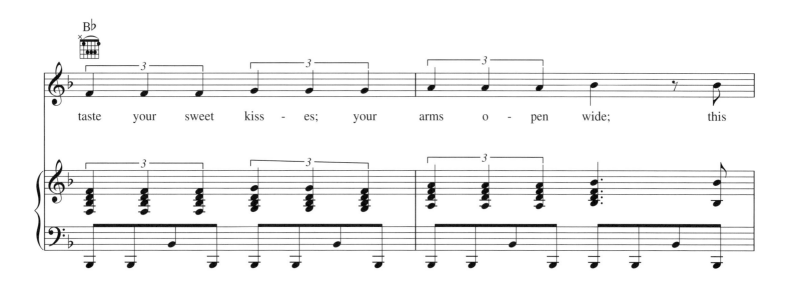

taste your sweet kiss - es; your arms o - pen wide; this

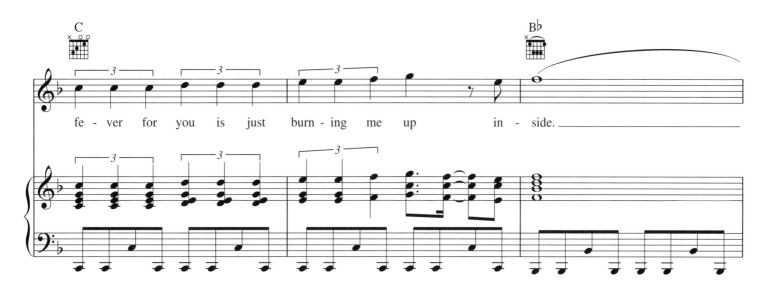

fe - ver for you is just burn - ing me up in - side.

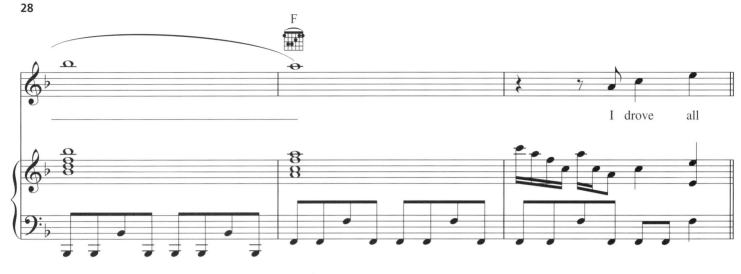

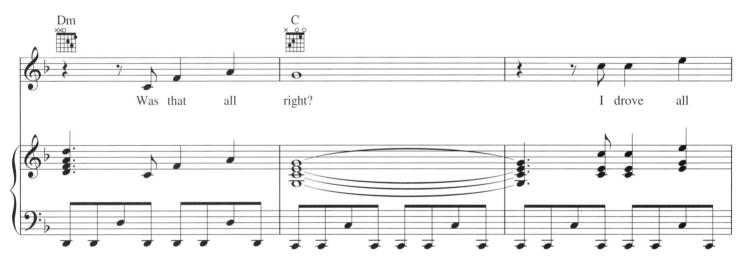

IN DREAMS

Words and Music by
ROY ORBISON

IT'S OVER

Words and Music by ROY ORBISON
and BILL DEES

MEAN WOMAN BLUES

Words and Music by
CLAUDE DeMETRUIS

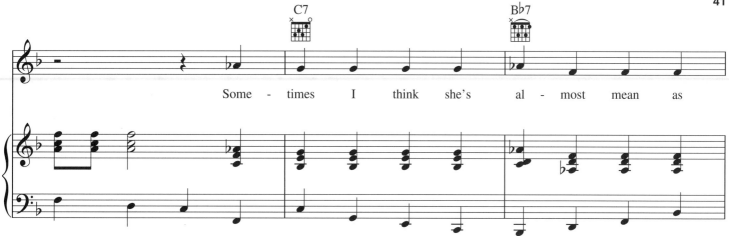

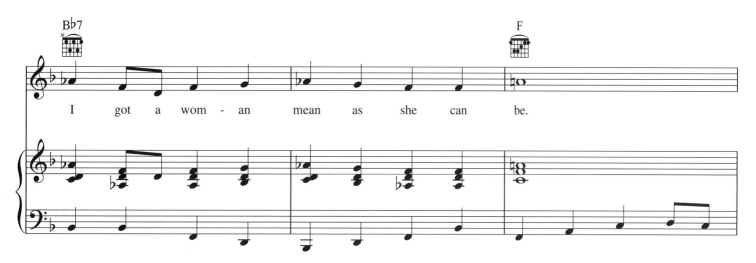

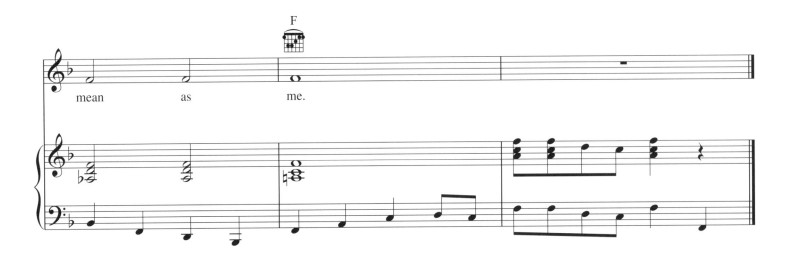

OH, PRETTY WOMAN

Words and Music by ROY ORBISON
and BILL DEES

Moderate Rock

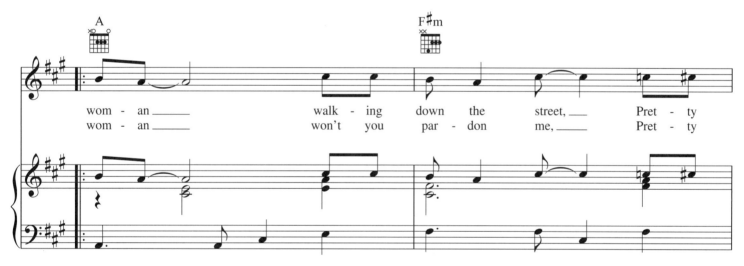

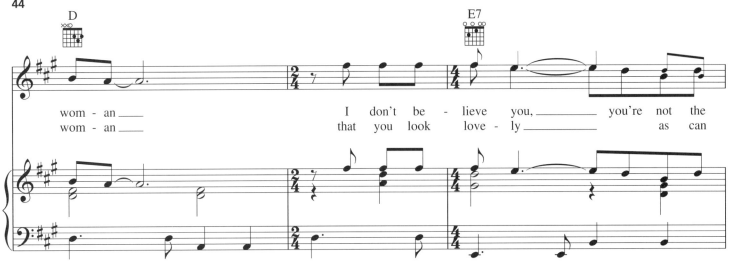

wom - an _____ I don't be - lieve you, _____ you're not the
wom - an _____ that you look love - ly _____ as can

truth No one could look as good as
be Are you lone - ly just like

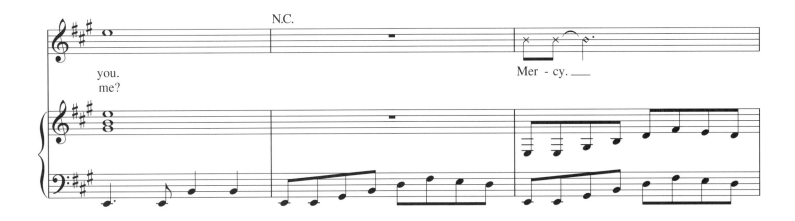

you. Mer - cy. _____
me?

Pret - ty

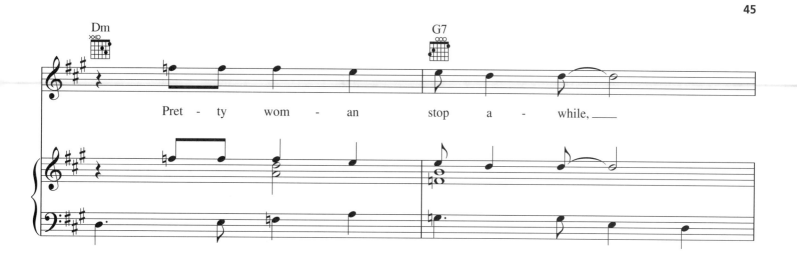

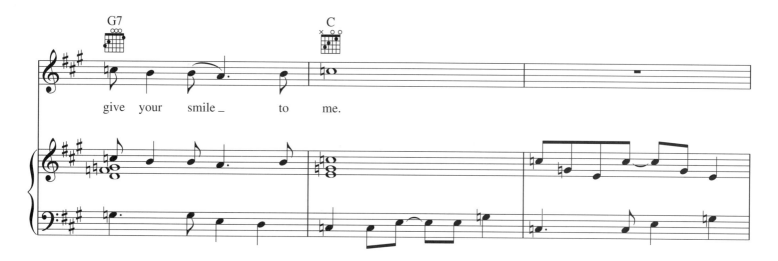

look my way, _____ Pret - ty wom - an

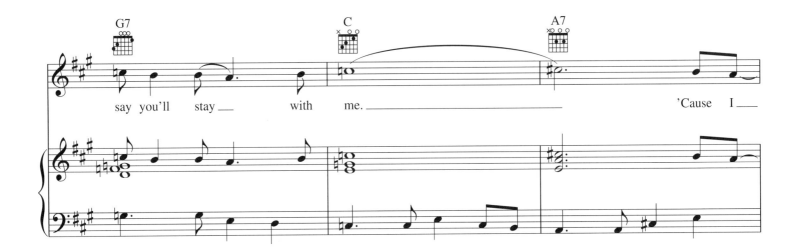

say you'll stay ___ with me. _____ 'Cause I ___

___ need you ___ I'll treat you right.

Come with me ba - by. ___ Be mine to -

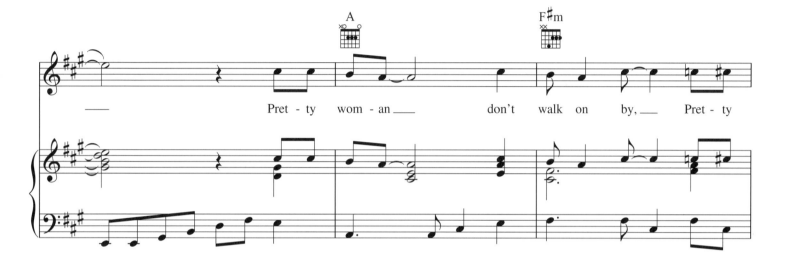

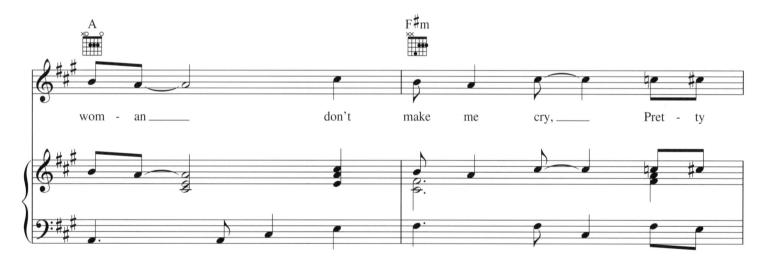

OOBY-DOOBY

Words and Music by WADE L. MOORE
and RICHARD A. PENNER

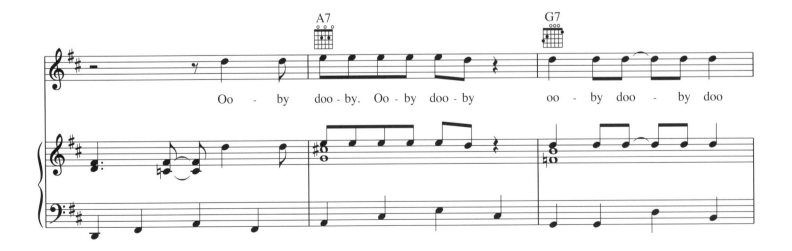

wah doo wah doo wah. ___ Well, you wig-gle to the left. You
wig-gle and you shake like a
you've been a strut-ting 'cause

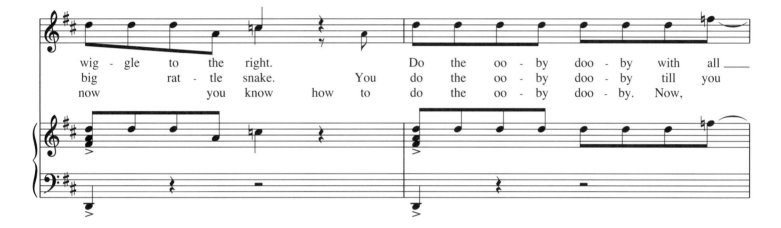

wig-gle to the right. Do the oo-by doo-by with all ___
big rat-tle snake. You do the oo-by doo-by till you
now you know how to do the oo-by doo-by. Now,

___ your might._ Oo-by doo-by.
think your heart will break. Oo-by doo-by. } Oo-by doo-by.
ba-by, let's go. Oo-by doo-by.

To Coda ⊕

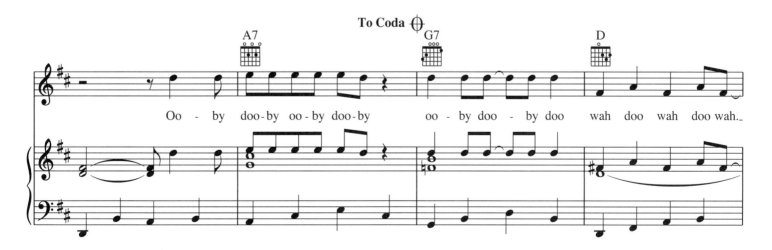

Oo-by doo-by oo-by doo-by oo-by doo-by doo wah doo wah doo wah._

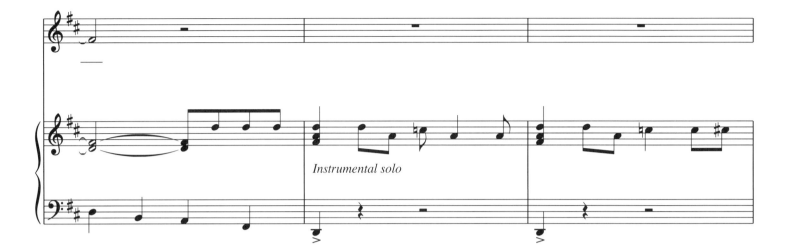

Instrumental solo

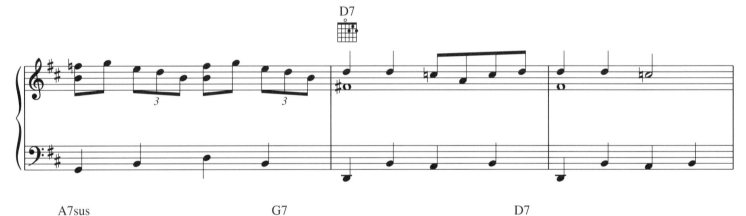

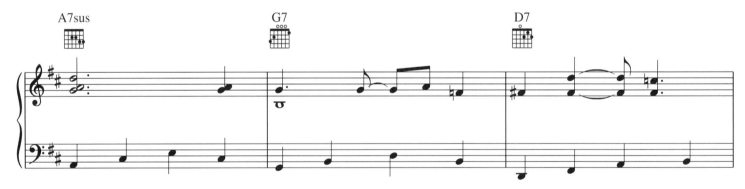

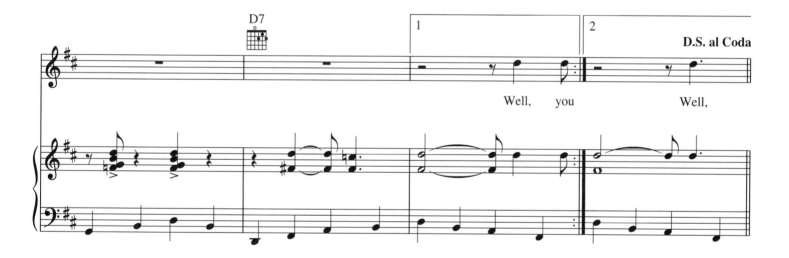

Well, you   Well,

doo - by doo - by doo wah doo wah doo wah. __

PRETTY ONE

Words and Music by
ROY ORBISON

Moderately

Hey there, _ pret - ty one, _ take a look at _ what you've done. _ You've

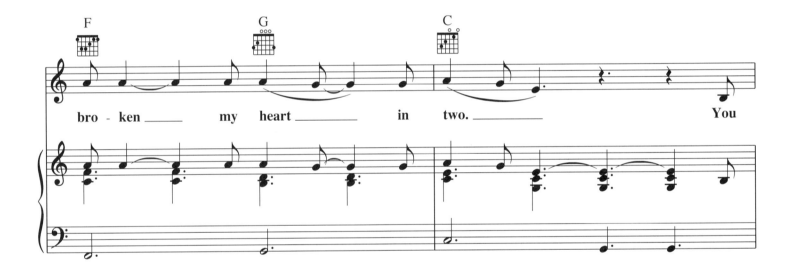

bro - ken _ my heart _ in two. _ You

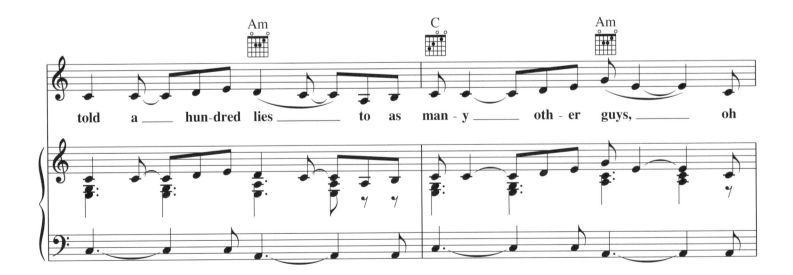

told a _ hun-dred lies _ to as man - y _ oth - er guys, _ oh

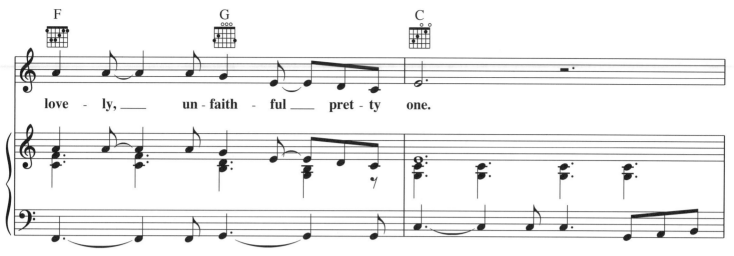

love - ly, __ un - faith - ful __ pret - ty one.

Some day, __ when you're old - er __ and your fu - ture __ has past, _____ you will

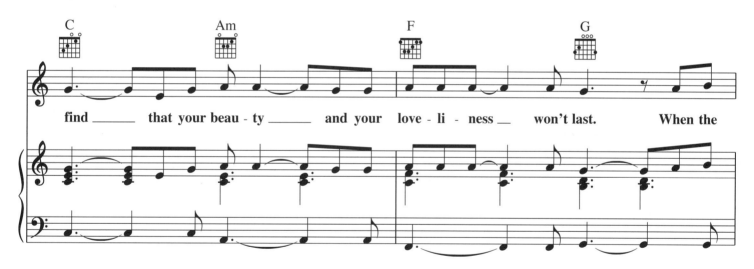

find _____ that your beau - ty _____ and your love - li - ness __ won't last. When the

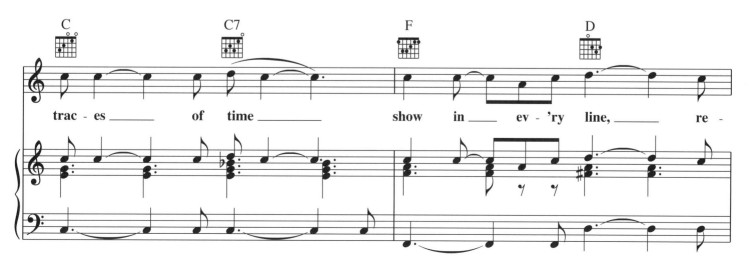

trac - es _____ of time _____ show in __ ev - 'ry line, _____ re -

mem - ber ___ I still love ___ you, ___ pret - ty one, _____ pret - ty one, _____ pret - ty

one. _____

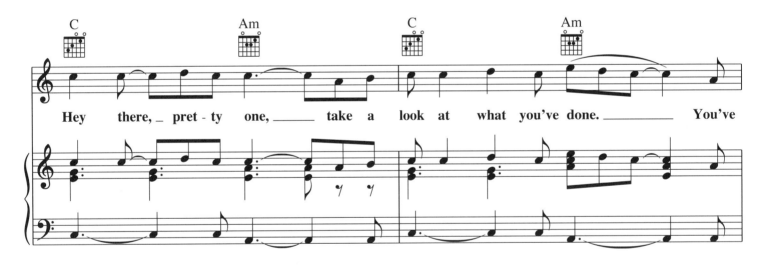

Hey there, ___ pret - ty one, _____ take a look at what you've done. _____ You've

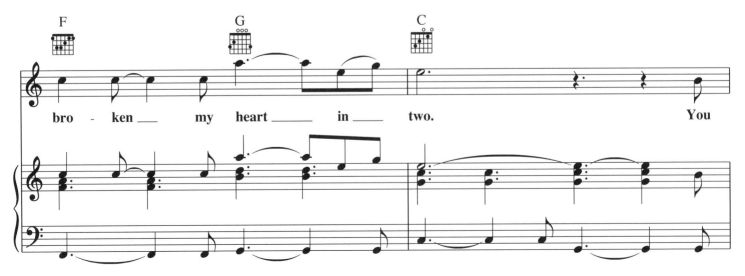

bro - ken ___ my heart _____ in ___ two. You

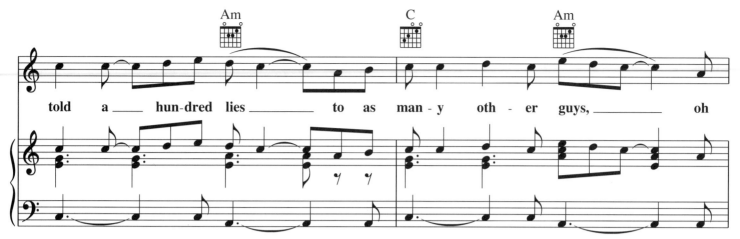

told a ___ hun-dred lies ___ to as man-y oth - er guys, _____ oh

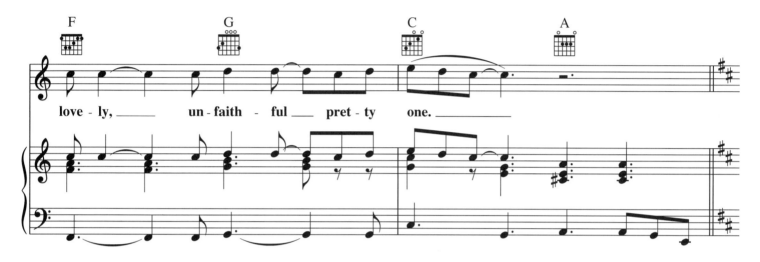

love - ly, _____ un-faith - ful ___ pret - ty one. _____

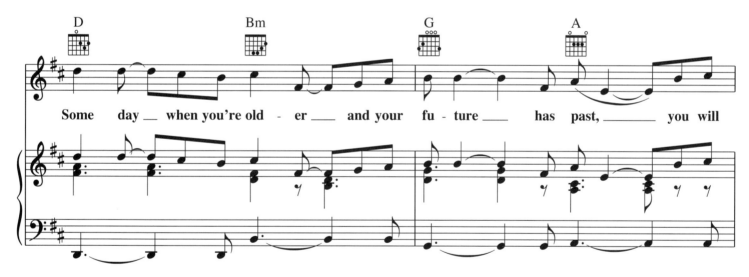

Some day ___ when you're old - er ___ and your fu - ture ___ has past, _____ you will

find _____ that your beau - ty ___ and your love - li - ness ___ won't last. When the

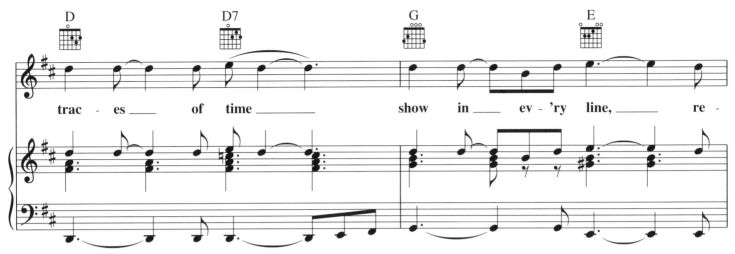

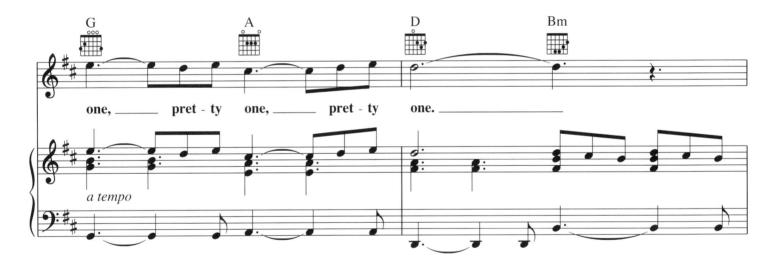

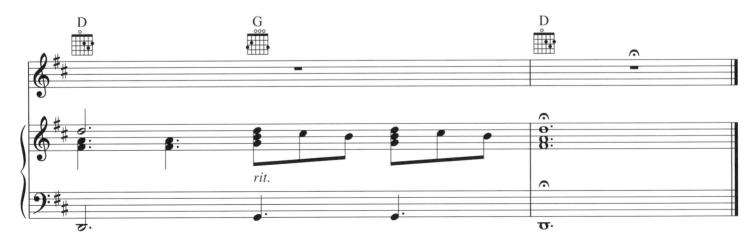

THAT LOVIN' YOU FEELIN' AGAIN

Words and Music by ROY ORBISON
and CHRIS PRICE

(Male:) When I saw you stand-ing there __ on the street, __ I found my-self by your

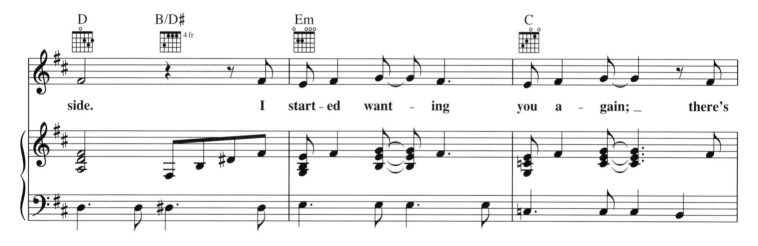

side. I start-ed want-ing you a-gain; __ there's

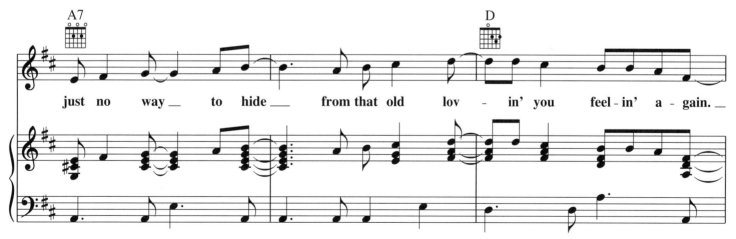

just no way __ to hide __ from that old lov-in' you feel-in' a-gain. __

It's real-ly got me reel-in' a - gain. ___ It on - ly seems to

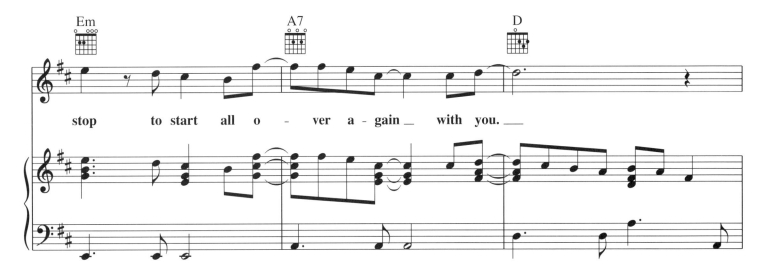

stop to start all o - ver a - gain ___ with you. ___

(Female:) I re-mem-ber how you al - ways ___ get that cer-tain look in your

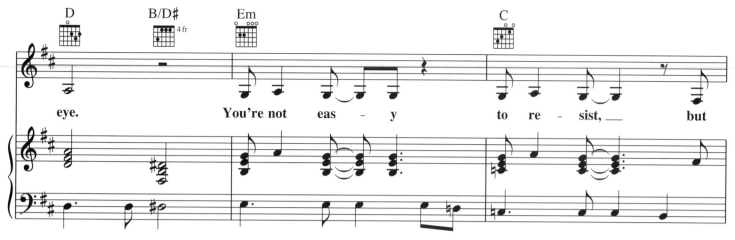

eye. You're not eas - y to re - sist, ___ but

I just walked _ on by ___ with that old lov - in' you feel - in' a - gain. ___

(lov - in' you feel - in') (lov - in' you)
___ It's real - ly got me reel - in' a - gain. ___ It on - ly seems to

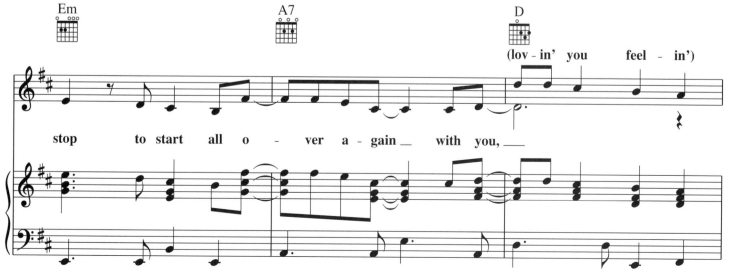

(lov - in' you feel - in')
stop to start all o - ver a - gain ___ with you, ___

(Male:) lov - in' you feel - in' with you. ___ (Male:) We were so

close. (Female:) We were too far a - part.

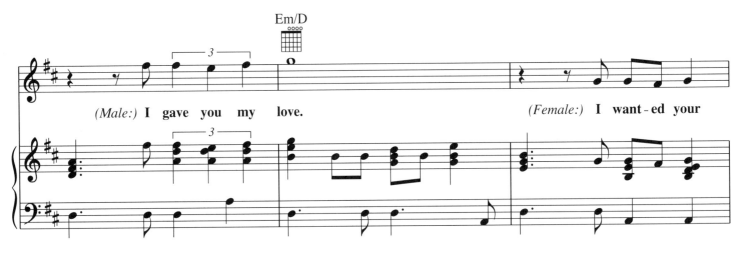

(Male:) I gave you my love. (Female:) I want - ed your

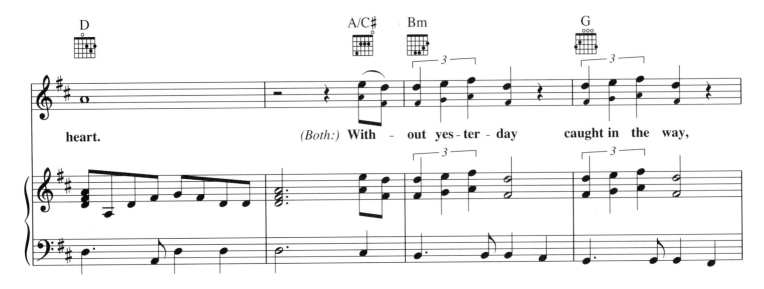

heart. (Both:) With - out yes - ter - day caught in the way,

may - be we'd still be to - geth - er, _____ shar -

- ing that lov-in' you feel-in' a - gain. _ It's real-ly got me reel-in' a - gain. _

_____ Will it ev - er stop and not start o - ver a - gain, _ that

lov - in' you feel-in' a - gain? _ No mat-ter how much _ I try, _

this lov-in' you feel-in' is why ___ it's

tak-en such a long, long time to say good-bye. ___ I'm get-ting

o - ver ___ you. ___ It's so hard to ___ do ___

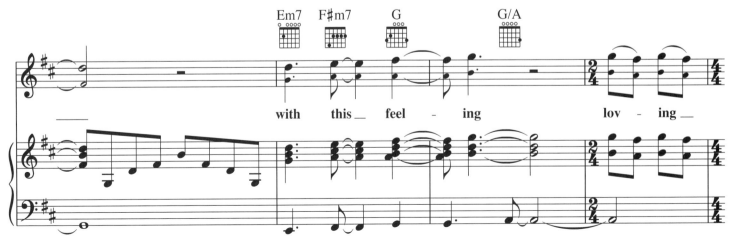

with this ___ feel - ing loving ___

you. _____ That

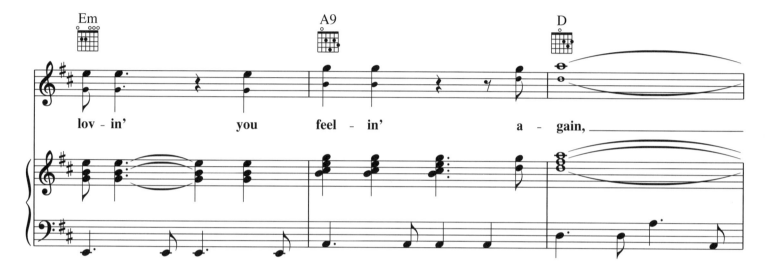

lov - in' you feel - in' a - gain, _____

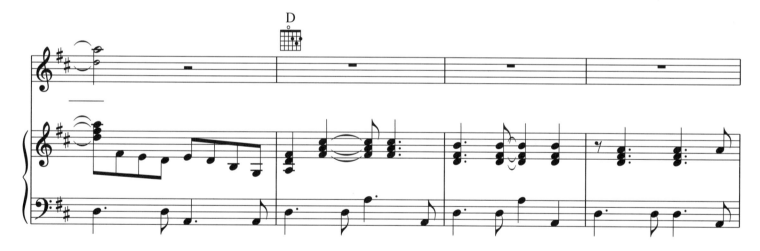

Repeat and Fade

lov - in' you feel - in' a - gain. ___ That

RUNNING SCARED

Words and Music by ROY ORBISON
and JOE MELSON

Just run - ning scared _____ each place we go, _____ so a - fraid _____ that he might show. Yeah, run - ning

WALK ON

Words and Music by ROY ORBISON
and BILL DEES

Moderately, in 2

far. _____ Quick-ly brush _____ a-

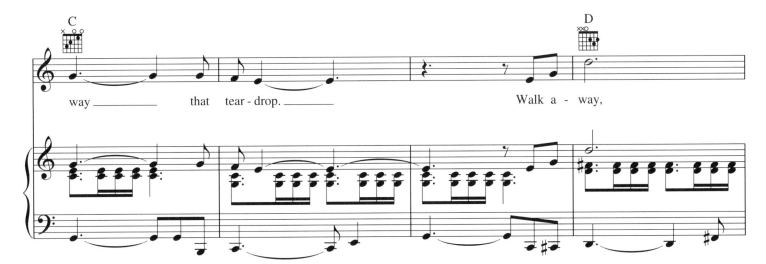

way _____ that tear-drop. _____ Walk a - way,

dar - ling; don't stop. _____ Don't look

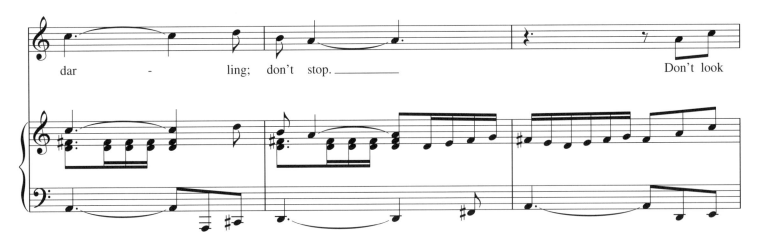

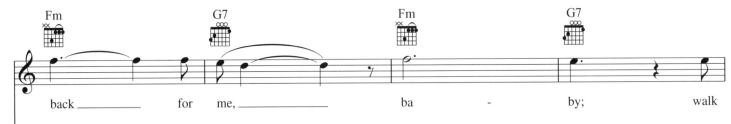

back _____ for me, _____ ba - by; walk

on. _____ Walk

on; don't turn a - round. _____

Walk on _____

to high-er ground. Take the

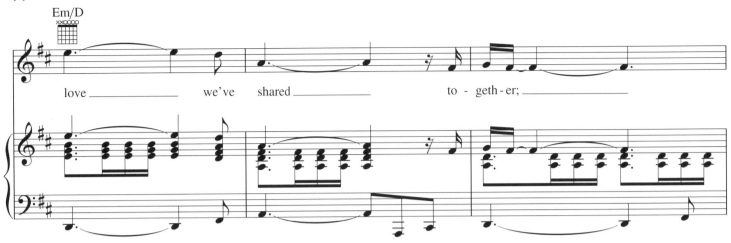

love _____ we've shared _____ to - geth - er; _____

keep it in _____ your heart for -

ev - er. _____ Don't for - get

me, but ba - by, walk

on. _____ If you

ev - er loved _____ me,

ba - by, walk

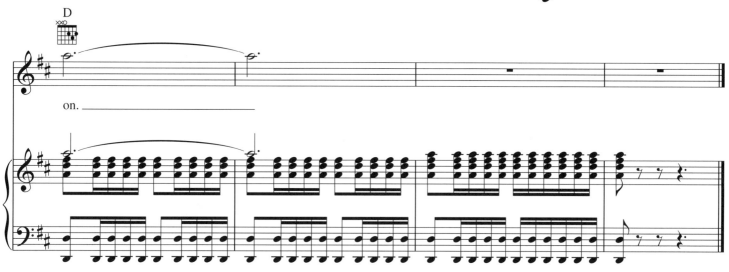

on. _____

WAYMORE'S BLUES

Words and Music by WAYLON JENNINGS
and CURTIS BUCK

Moderately, in 2

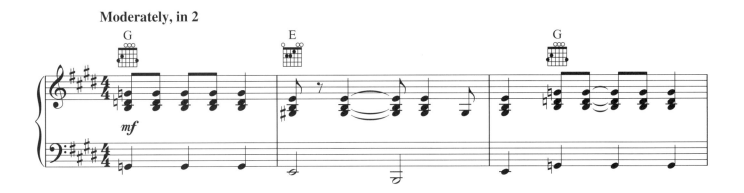

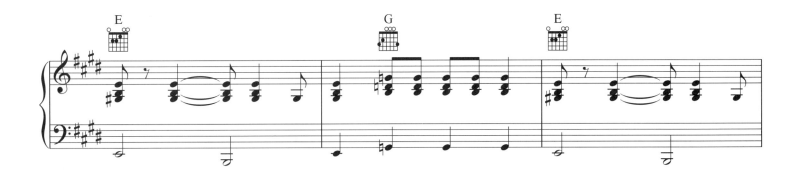

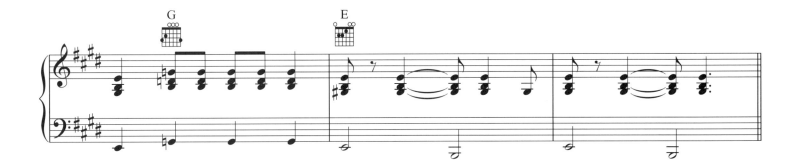

Ear - ly one morn - ing, it was driz - zl - ing rain. ___ You got to
wan - na get to heav - en, you got - ta D - I - E. ___ You got to
Lord - y, have ___ mer - cy! What's the mat - ter with me? ___ What

'Round the curve ___ come the Mem - phis ___ train. ___
put on your coat and your T - I - E. ___ If you
makes me wan - na love ev - 'ry wom - an I see? ___ A -

Heard some - bod - y hol - ler, and a mil - lion more, ___ "The
wan - na catch a rab - bit in an L - O - G, ___ you got - ta
rag - in' when I met her; ___ a - rag - in' a - gain.

king is dead, ___ but Lord, he still ain't gone. ___ Lord, he
make a com - mo - tion like a D - O - G, ___ like a
Ev - 'ry - one I see, just like the place I came in, ___ like the

A7

still ain't ___ gone.
D - O - G.
place I came in. (Hot dog!) ___

Well, he still ain't __ gone. (My God, __ my God, __
Like a D - O - G. (Oh, yes, __ yes, like __
Like the place I came

__ he still __ ain't __ gone.) __   If you
__ a D - O - G.) __   Good __

in.   (The place I came in.) __

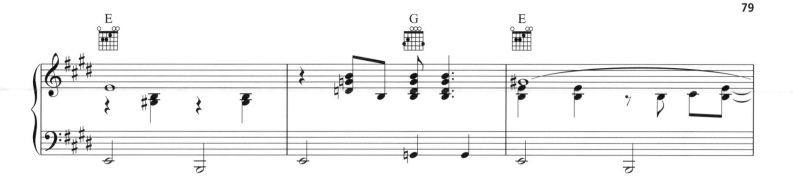

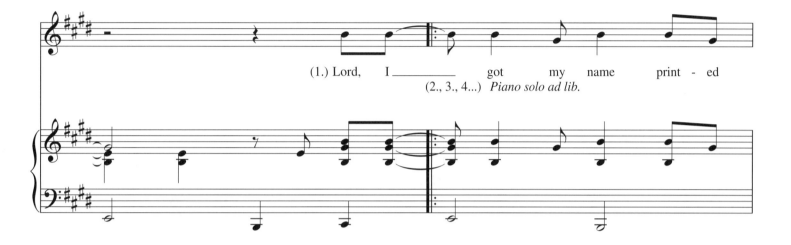

(1.) Lord, I _____ got my name print - ed
(2., 3., 4...) *Piano solo ad lib.*

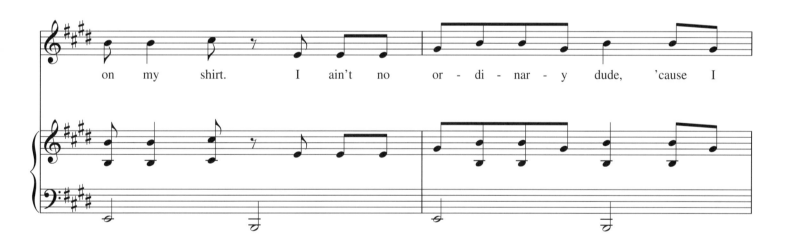

on my shirt. I ain't no or - di - nar - y dude, 'cause I

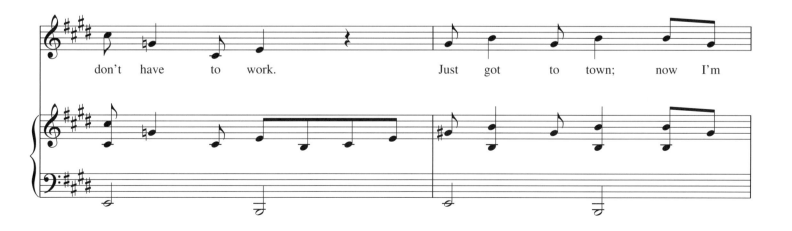

don't have to work. Just got to town; now I'm

gone a-gain.___ But it's a dif-fer-ent track,___ but it's the

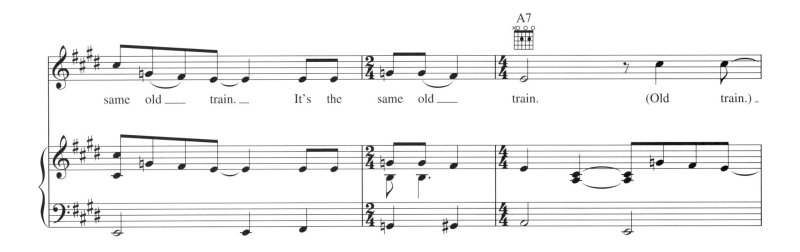

same old ___ train.___ It's the same old ___ train. (Old train.) ___

___ It's the same old ___

train. (Oh, Lord, ___ my God, ___ it's the same ___ old ___ train.) ___

Repeat ad lib. and Fade

Optional Ending

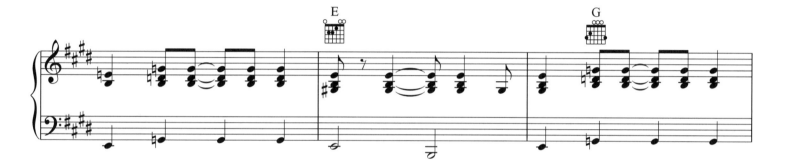

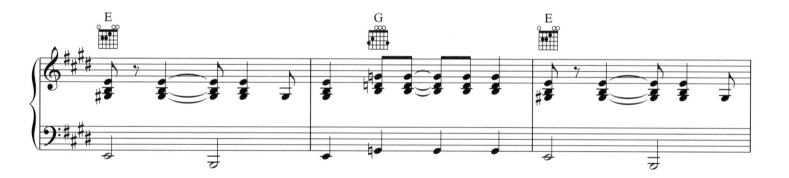

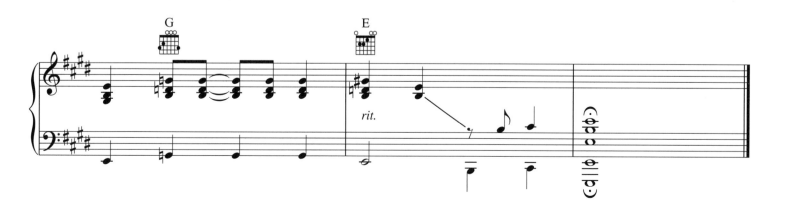

WHAT'D I SAY

Words and Music by
RAY CHARLES

Moderately fast

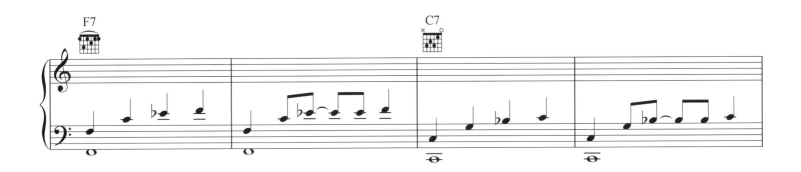

Hey,   ma - ma,   don't   you
See   the   wom - an   with   the
See   the   wom - an   with   the

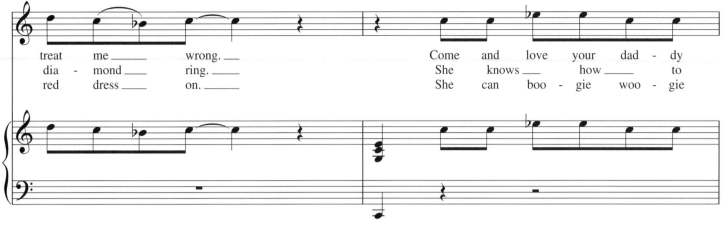

treat me _____ wrong. _____ Come and love your dad - dy
dia - mond _____ ring. _____ She knows _____ how _____ to
red dress _____ on. _____ She can boo - gie woo - gie

all night _ long. _
shake that _ thing. _ } All _____ right, _ hey, _
all night _ long. _

hey, all _ right, oh, _____ all right. _

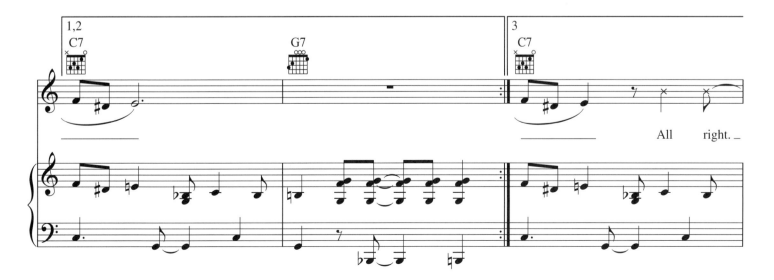

_____ _____ All right. _

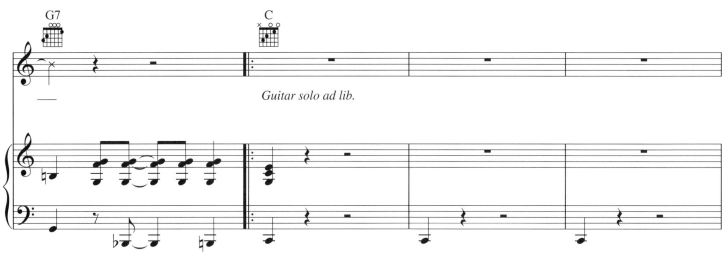

Guitar solo ad lib.

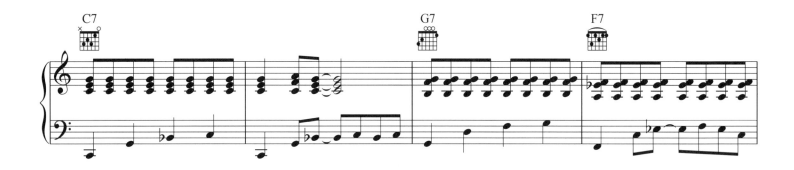

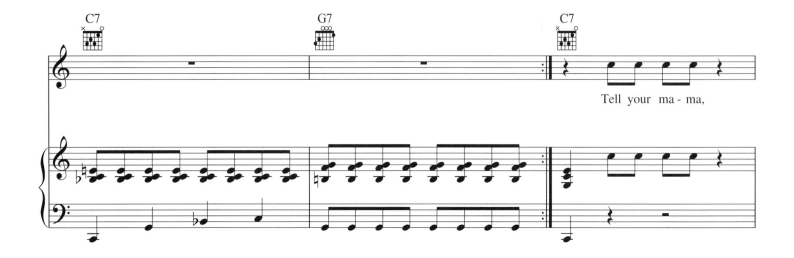

Tell your ma - ma,

tell your pa, gon - na send you back to Ar - kan - sas. ___ Oh,

F7   **C7**

ho, ___ hey, ___ hey,

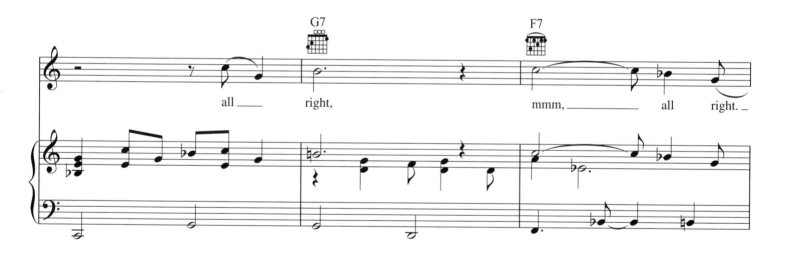

G7   **F7**

all ___ right, mmm, ___ all right. _

C7   **G7**   **C7**

___ Tell me, what'd I say? ___ Oh,

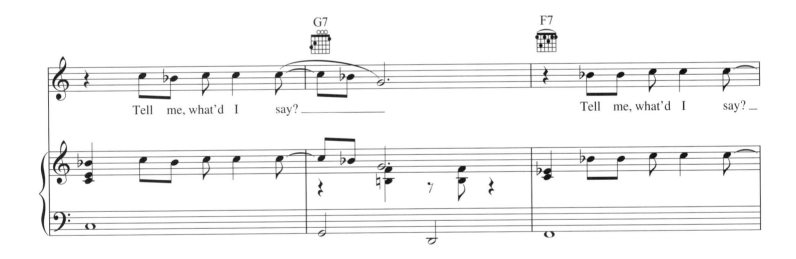

Yeah, I wan - na know. ___ Ba - by, I wan - na know. ___

Yeah, I wan - na know. ___

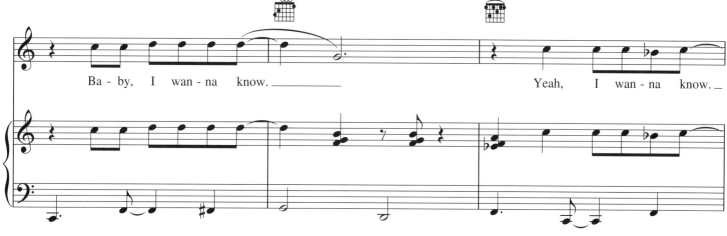

Ba - by, I wan - na know. ___ Yeah, I wan - na know. ___

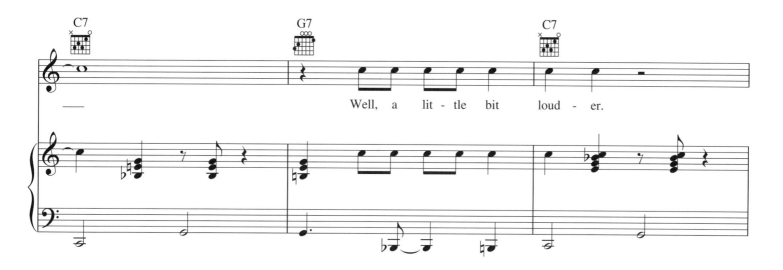

Well, a lit - tle bit loud - er.

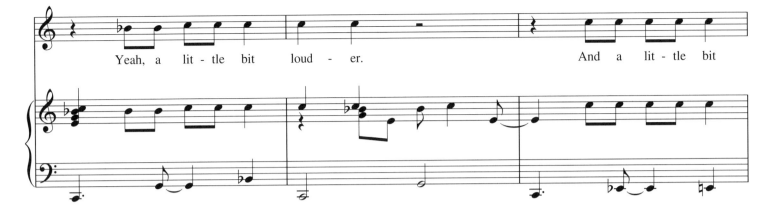

Yeah, a lit-tle bit loud - er. And a lit-tle bit

loud - er. And a lit-tle bit loud - er.

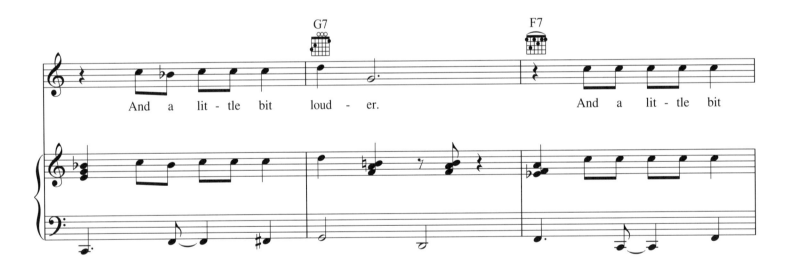

And a lit-tle bit loud - er. And a lit-tle bit

loud - er. Tell me, what'd I say? ___

Tell me, what'd I _____ say? ____

Tell me, what'd I _____ say? _

Tell me, what'd I _____ say? ____

Tell me, what'd I _____ say? ____

Tell me, what'd I _____ say. _

Tell me, what'd I _____ say? _____

YOU GOT IT

Words and Music by ROY ORBISON,
JEFF LYNNE and TOM PETTY

Moderately

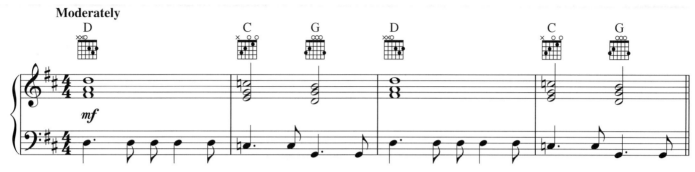

Ev-'ry time I look in-to your lov-ing eyes _____
Ev-'ry time I hold you I be-gin to un-der-stand. _____

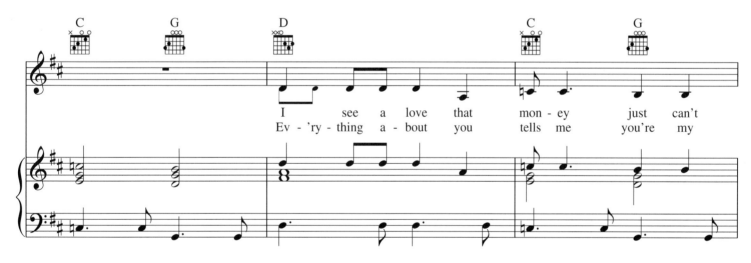

I see a love that mon-ey just can't
Ev-'ry-thing a-bout you tells me you're my

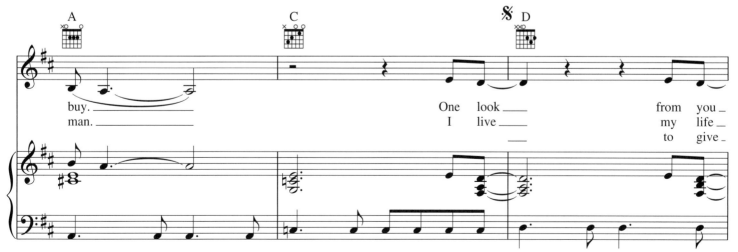

buy.
man. _____

One look _____ from you _____
I live _____ my life _____
to give _____

I drift _____ a - way. _____ I pray _____
to be _____ with you. _____ No one _____
my love _____ to you. _____ I know _

that you _____ are here _____ to stay. _
can do _____ the things _____ you do. _
you feel _____ the way _____ I do. _

To Coda ⊕

An - y - thing you want, _____ you got it.

An - y - thing you need, _____ you got it. An - y - thing at all, _

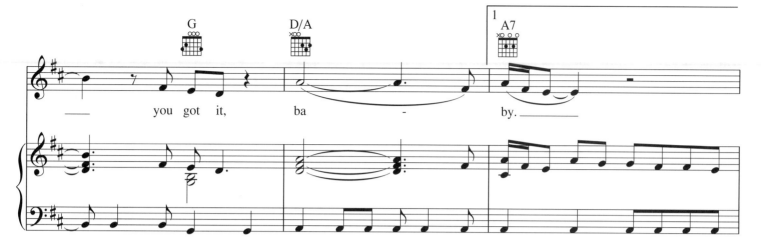

you got it, ba - by. ____

by. ____

An - y - thing you want, ____ an - y - thing you need, ___

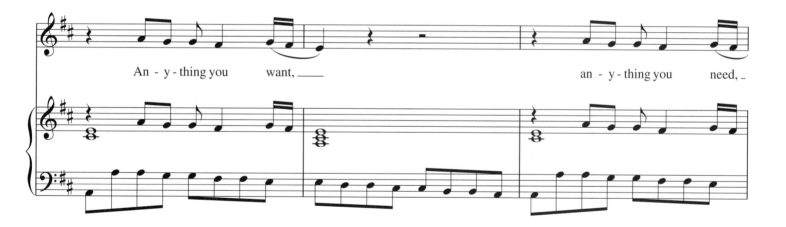

an - y - thing at all. ____

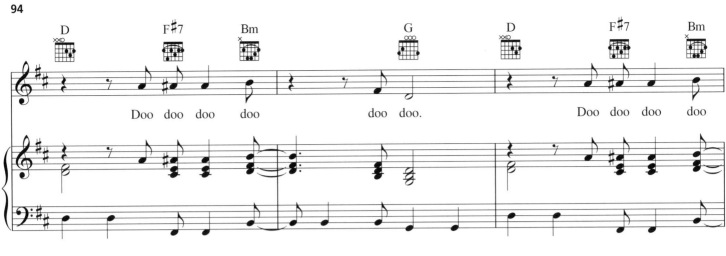

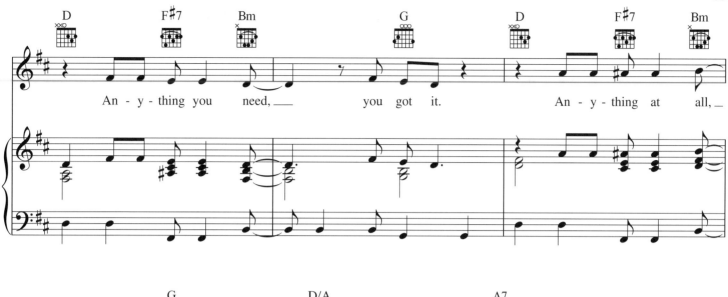

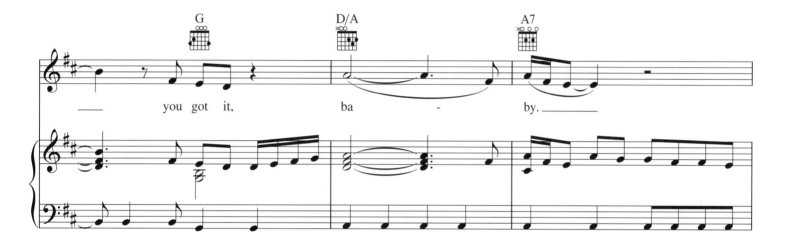

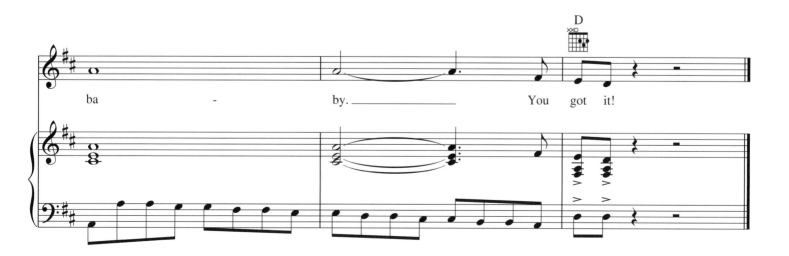

WORKING FOR THE MAN

Words and Music by
ROY ORBISON

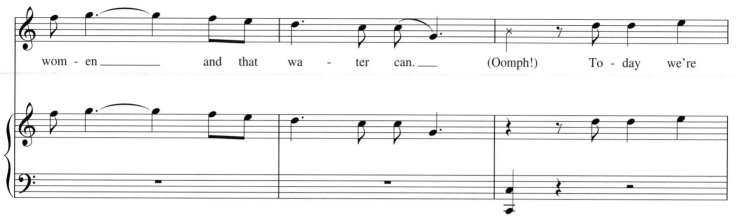

wom - en _____ and that wa - ter can. ___ (Oomph!) To - day we're

Moderately fast, steadily

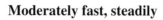

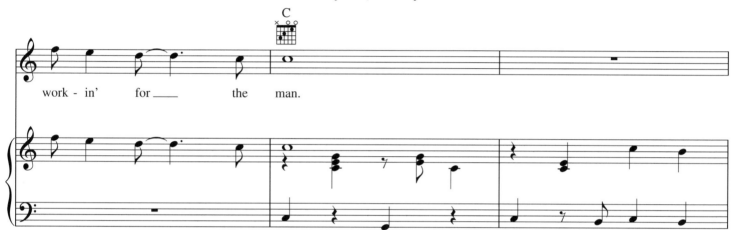

work - in' for ____ the man.

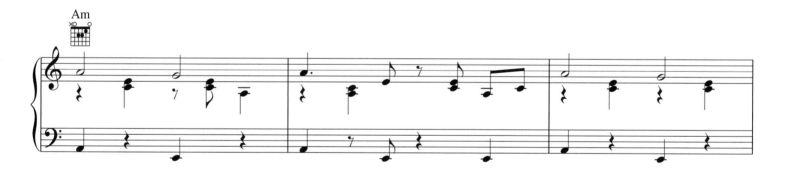

Well, pick up your feet; we've got a
pick - ing 'em up, and I'm a -

dead - line to meet.   I'm gon - na see you make it on ___
lay - ing 'em down.   I   be - lieve ___ he's ___ gon - na work me

time. ___   Oh,   don't re - lax;   I want
in - to the ground. _   I   pull to the left;   I _____

el - bows and backs.   I wan - na see ev - 'ry - bod - y from be -
heave to the right.   I ought - ta kill him, but it would - n't be ___

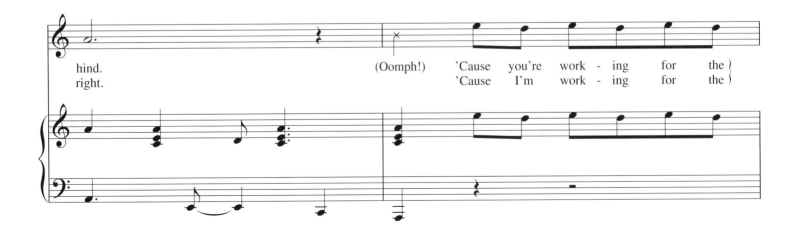

hind.   (Oomph!) 'Cause you're work - ing for the
right.   'Cause I'm work - ing for the

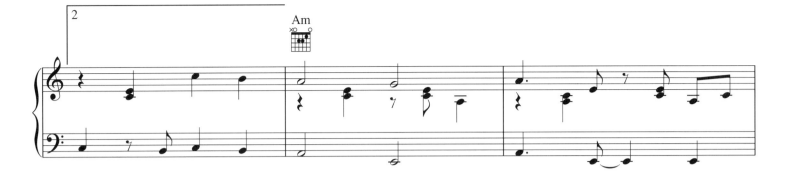

Well, the boss man's daugh - ter sneaks -

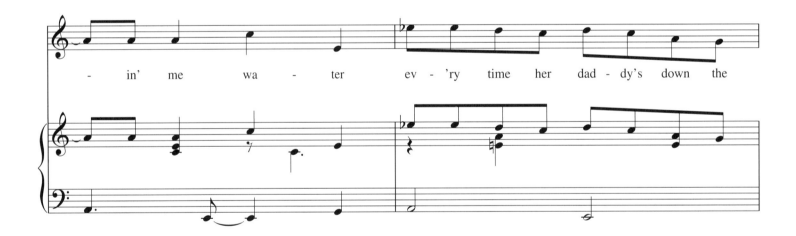

- in' me wa - ter ev - 'ry time her dad - dy's down the

line. She says, "A - meet me to - night, _ love - a - me right, _ and

man. _____ I got-ta make him a hand. _____

Repeat and Fade

A - work - ing for the man. _____

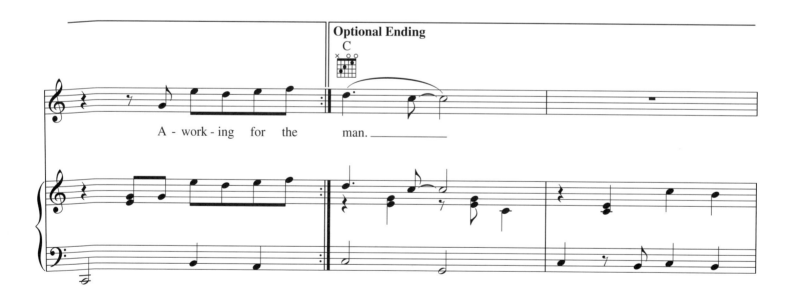

Optional Ending

A - work - ing for the man. _____